COUNT THE WAVES

ALSO BY SANDRA BEASLEY

Don't Kill the Birthday Girl: Tales from an Allergic Life
I Was the Jukebox: Poems
Theories of Falling: Poems

COUNT THE WAVES

Poems

Sandra Beasley

Sandra Beasley

For David —
With gratitude for this conversation
in DC, and for your incredible
work — looking forward
to delving deeper.
Cheers, *SB*

W. W. NORTON & COMPANY

Independent Publishers Since 1923

New York • London

For information about permission to reproduce selections from this book,
write to Permissions, W. W. Norton & Company, Inc.,
500 Fifth Avenue, New York, NY 10110

For information about special discounts for bulk purchases, please contact
W. W. Norton Special Sales at specialsales@wwnorton.com or 800-233-4830

Manufacturing by Courier Westford
Production manager: Louise Mattarelliano

Library of Congress Cataloging-in-Publication Data

Beasley, Sandra.
[Poems. Selections]
Count the waves : poems / Sandra Beasley.—First edition.
pages ; cm
ISBN 978-0-393-24320-8 (hardcover)
I. Title.
PS3602.E2558A6 2015
811'.6—dc23

2014047938

ISBN 978-0-393-35321-1

W. W. Norton & Company, Inc.
500 Fifth Avenue, New York, N.Y. 10110
www.wwnorton.com

W. W. Norton & Company Ltd.
15 Carlisle Street, London W1D 3BS

1 2 3 4 5 6 7 8 9 0

for Champneys,
and travels to come

CONTENTS

ACKNOWLEDGMENTS

I am grateful to editors of the journals in which versions of these poems appeared: *32 Poems, AGNI, Black Warrior Review, Blackbird, Cave Wall, Copper Nickel, The Gettysburg Review, The Iowa Review, the minnesota review, The Oxford American, Poetry, Ploughshares, The Rattling Wall, The Rumpus, Seneca Review, Tin House,* and *Virginia Quarterly Review.*

"The Wake" won the 2006 Elinor Benedict Poetry Prize from Northern Michigan University. "Instantaneous Letter Writer" (as "Mercy") was published in a letterpress broadside edition by the Kalamazoo Book Arts Center. "Economy" and "Grief Puppet" were featured in the Academy of American Poets Poem-a-Day series. "Halloween" was featured in *The Chronicle Review* "Monday's Poem" blog, written by Lisa Russ Spaar. "American Caution" was part of the Buck Downs "Literary Picks of the Week" series. "One-Tenth of the Body" won the 2012 Larry Neal Writers' Award from the DC Commission on the Arts and Humanities, and is part of the *District Lines* anthology from Politics & Prose. "Let Me Count the Waves" and "The Editor of *Encyclopædia Britannica* Regrets Everything" are part of *The Incredible Sestina Anthology*, edited by Daniel Nester.

A selection of these poems won the 2013 Center for Book Arts Chapbook Competition, judged by Harryette Mullen and Sharon Dolin, and were published in a letterpress edition as

"None in the Same Room: Poems from *The Traveler's Vade Mecum*."

I am grateful to the Virginia Center for Creative Arts, the Sewanee Writers' Conference, the Jentel Artist Residency, Lenoir-Rhyne University, Cornell College, and the DC Commission on the Arts and Humanities, for providing fellowships and financial aid during periods critical to the completion of this collection.

Thanks to the folks at W. W. Norton, particularly my editor Jill Bialosky. Thanks to Helen Klein Ross for the anthology solicitation that sparked the *Traveler's Vade Mecum* project. This collection wouldn't have coalesced without camaraderie and readership from JC, MT, HL, KD, NEI, MM, MJ, EM, HJ, and others. As always, I'm indebted to my family—particularly my sister, mother, and father—for their love and support.

COUNT THE WAVES

How do I love thee? Let me count the ways.

—Elizabeth Barrett Browning

Sonnets from the Portuguese, 1850

INNER FLAMINGO

At night my body discovers
her secret geometries—
inner-flamingo knee hitch,
inner-flamenco arm arch,
Hermes' diagonal of flight
across the mattress.

The sleeping body is selfish.
The sleeping body cannot lie.

Once there was the man
from whom I always woke
huddled at the bed's edge.
Then there was a man who
laid his lust as a doorknocker
at the small of my back.

The first time I laid down
with you—sweat-stuck,

each onioned in the skin
of the other—I assumed
the unconscious hours

would peel us free. Yet
when sun cracked its eye
over the horizon, we were as

we'd been. And the pink of me
cocked her head, listening.

In 1853, A. C. Baldwin published a compendium of phrases that could be referenced by number, a code for conversation over long distances. He called this *The Traveler's Vade Mecum; or Instantaneous Letter Writer, by Mail or Telegraph, for the Convenience of Persons Traveling on Business or for Pleasure, and for Others, Whereby a Vast Amount of Time, Labor, and Trouble Is Saved.*

THE TRAVELER'S VADE MECUM, LINE #907: "THE EXHIBITION WAS VERY BEAUTIFUL"

The exhibition opened on a rainy Thursday, with cello suite.

They hung the paintings to be viewed from both front and back.

Luna moths flapped their great green sail-wings.

Stingrays flapped their great gray sail-wings.

Those visiting the exhibition were encouraged to touch.

Captions were available in Braille and audio.

The exhibition tasted like cherries.

A critic asked if the exhibition was a "facile juxtaposition of ideals."

The mother of the exhibition calls constantly and the father, never.

The exhibition has taken to pouring a little scotch in the coffee.

When designing layout, remember

it is crucial how a bias cut fits at the exhibition's hips

and foot traffic turns to the right, not the left.

They hung the sculptures to be viewed from both above and below.

They painted the walls a shade of "eggshell, minus calcium."

The exhibition did not consider itself an exhibitionist

until the incident at the east window.

The exhibition is very sorry and will refund upon request.

Stingrays flapped their great gray sail-wings.

Luna moths flapped their great green sail-wings.

No matter how short a trip, the exhibition packs two pairs of shoes.

The exhibition never knows when it is going home again.

THE TRAVELER'S VADE MECUM, LINE #1366: "NOTHING BUT CASH WILL ANSWER"

On the fifteenth of February, the old man set his bag of coins on the bank's counter. The teller informed him it was no longer money. The bag of coins had ceased to be money exactly ten years and six weeks prior. He looked at her. He had a sibilant breath, each exhale hissing slightly against his teeth. She slid the Decimal Currency Board's pamphlet over the counter and suggested, not unkindly, that a collector might buy the coins. That night, he spread them out on the table and ordered them by year. Sea levels rose and fell behind Britannia. The lighthouse collapsed; the ship sailed on. The monarchs switched the direction of their gaze. Britannia became a chattering wren. FAR THING each coin promised. By then, there was no brandy left in the house.

THE TRAVELER'S VADE MECUM, LINE #6682: "IN AN OFFICIAL CAPACITY"

Because you gave it to me
I had to eat it, husk
gritting its way through my gut;

because I gave it to you
you had to wear it, the wool
tacky and stiff with fat.

In this way we understand
each other. What can I tell you?
I await my orders. You await

my orders. My child writes
of his new toy, a gyroscope,
pregnant with unspun energy.

From two seas over I try
to thread the string. Once
I went to the house of a chief

great among my people.
He had one souvenir: bone
chipped from a warrior's socket.

He smoothed it over and over
with his thumb. *Nothing*
they give you will mean anything,

he said. *It has to be taken*
to mean anything. My friend,
when the slug punches

into your lung, what sound will
your men make as they flee back
to the trees? This new world

will not wait forever. It sits
on its spindle, strung tight.
It slickens your daughter's skin
as she rises from the lake.

THE TRAVELER'S VADE MECUM, LINE #1015: "PLEASE COME IN THE BOAT OF TO-DAY"

Beneath whitewash, beneath brick, beneath mud,
fourteen boats of Abydos row toward eternity.
No bodies here—only the ghost-shit of ants,
who consume the hulls but leave the shape behind.
Each timber tongues its neighbor, tenon to mortise,
with nothing but rope to hold them together.
No pegs, no joists.
Who builds a boat like that?

Only those expecting to unbuild boats like that,
to stack the tamarix planks on their heads,
to walk seventy miles to the Red Sea in search of
trade. *Fair* is a human conceit. Priests know this.
Carpenters know this. They bundle the reeds
anyway, packing seams tight for an intended tide.
They cut planks from cedar with a deep taproot
that salts the earth around itself, and will not burn.

THE EMPEROR'S VALENTINE

I admit, the monkeys were overkill.
They refused to leave their jeweled hats alone.
They hurled the grapes at each other like small,
hard promises of sex to come. With wild
animals there is always a small, hard
promise of sex to come. Even turtles,
shells scraping as they circle their turtle
tank. For us, sharing a glass house would kill
the spark. But they're exhibitionists. Hard
to make blush, turtles. Never bathed alone,
using the same dish to drink. In the wild,
my dear, I would ask for only the small
favors: grooming you with my teeth, your small
hands tugging my hair, gently as turtles
tug mouthfuls of watercress from the wild.
We can forget that to eat is to kill,
with chewing so elegant. But alone—
thinking you're alone—I see you bite hard
at the fatty bones of the chicken, hard
at the apple's core, licking the dismal
buttery bits from the knife. It's a lone
wolf way to eat and Empress, this turtle
heart questions its shell. It's kill or be killed,

watching you chew. Yes, those monkeys were wild
but they were on to something, being wild,
refusing to butler, stomping the hard
grapes to wine even as guards came to kill
them. To determine one's death is the small
victory of caged beasts; even the turtle
in a cat's mouth can draw up, die alone.
Surrounded by servants, I feel alone.
The lions do not comfort me; the wild
gazelles do not distract me. The turtles
in their endless rutting seem small and hard;
and your heart, in its rut, seems hard and small.
Loosen your robes. Whether you kiss or kill
your emperor, free him from this lone, hard
bed. My room grows wild with vines big and small,
and turtles with nothing but time to kill.

THE WAKE

James Abbott McNeill Whistler

~

Huddled in the gondola, tired of numb fumbling
with plate and stylus, he abandons the eleventh etching
for dovebelly brown paper and the swipe of chalk.

The laundrettes have come down to the doorway,
dipping their wicker baskets into the water.
A balcony above divulges their linens.

His betrothed Rialto, all state and arch, is waiting.
But his line wants to stay here and seduce this alley,
occupy each molded shadow of stairstep. Shiver thin

then thick. Caress the bend of waists slendered by work.
The girls fold sheets corner to corner. They stretch
and blend. When the color comes it is arterial,

cut wrist let loose upon the world—
brick ochred mandarin, windowpanes frocked
olive green, a sky fleshed with morning—

until a crowd of starlings descends on the balustrade.
He picks up the black charcoal, starts to adulterate
pink horizon with their chattering forms. Stops.

The girls, they are finishing now, they are yawning,
and the gondolier mutters for his lunch.
As they pull away from the canal's slick edge

the water holds, for a breath, the shape of their passing.
He knows no plate could manage that wet cleave,
no pastel give more than the dimmest echo

of that blue lack. Thank god it is only a moment
before the sea is again seamless, complete. Something
he can honor. Something he can own.

Trixie's cough was a poor thread—slender, inconsistent—
something to worry about over the dinner roast, something
to pull loose with Darjeeling tea and honey. She poured

and pulled and out it came, and out, and out, into full ropes
that draped her. A rosary of hacking. Then they knew
a deeper thing, something bone-bred, had unraveled.

Nights like this he walks home through Hampstead Heath.
She sleeps, cushioned in gold velvet long worn away at the arms,
limp stitchwork dangling from one palm. He is ink-stained,

freezing, and still the silk jutting from his pocket matches
the band on his hat. A man of precision. He wishes
he could warm her, a blanket of muscle striated with gin,

but she can no longer manage the stairs to the bedroom.
Once, the Duveneck boys would have had a card game going.
Once he'd have called Maud, who oiled her breasts in lavender,

who knew the price at which each plate sells. But tonight
he pulls his own chair to his wife's and takes out the sketchpad.
He sets aside blue and white, sharpens yellow and gray.

Just as he drew the palazzo from its crumbling dock,
beadstringers from their murky alley, so he lifts her body
beyond a room of dirty porcelain and leather.

He traces the scape of her, calves lithe and unspent.
He crosses her ankles. He is humming, intent,
but she does not stir. A spider's line for her hair—skittering,

loose, black charcoal spinning itself away. He is
her own best hangman. He will call it by her name.
He will not fill in the cocoon of her face.

FIDELITY (II)

In some versions his pericardium
was pierced, the body bleeding water;
some say only the usual red.
In one story a full moon;
in another, hours of eclipse.
Where gospels agree

                  is at the door
of the cave, when a boulder rolls back
and some woman, one Mary or another,
names that first essential absence.

It is April, and he raises his fears
every three days. He brings home
a bouquet of muscular lilies. He waits
for the miracle.

               She calls her name
into a cave, and the cave answers with
her name.

THE TRAVELER'S VADE MECUM, LINE #4983: "HOW LONG AGO WAS IT?"

The seams of our gold world weaken—
gussets fray under the arms of the post office,
and the oriole's throat loosens its embroidery.

There are two ways a world can be edged:
with selvage, as a weft retreats
into itself, or with a marrying stitch.

Hurry, tailors.
Thread the needle of your bodies,
gather and placket. Hem the peach's flesh

where the stone pulled free. I
can only watch as each sequin of water
dissolves at your touch. But still,

skirt the shore in its ocean.
Clothe the house in its roof.
There is a threadbare spot in the eastern canopy—

You, lift the bobbin. You, measure the cut.
Don't look down, tailor.
Steady the hand that dares mend a sky.

The Traveler's Vade Mecum, Line #6746: "I Wish You to Adopt Pacific Measures"

You must set your watch back by three angers.

You must cultivate a vale of lilacs in your spleen.

An acid eats, yet we do not praise its appetite.

A wound has lips but they do not speak of love.

THE TRAVELER'S VADE MECUM, LINE #7671: "IT IS NO SECRET HERE"

Dirt, wrote a British anthropologist,
is matter out of place. Drop a grape
from bowl to table and we call it *dirty.*
Drop a grape to the floor and it is *trash.*
Bowl, table: these are ordering agents,
ways to tell the functional from fallen.

Skin, tendon: these are ordering agents.

You want to kiss my mouth, but not
the teeth inside my mouth. You want
to hold my hand, but not the blood
within that hand. There is a truth
in you, but it won't be the dirty truth
until it tumbles into the air between
us. In this city, there is always
a long walk home in 7 a.m. light,
high heels stabbing the subway grates.
A walk home past gutters littered
with the non sequitur of chicken bones,
wings that once held a dream of flight.

KING

Among the blind, the one-eyed man is king.

This vexes the one-eyed man, who'd hoped to
play upright bass for a living. He loves
that four-string simplicity, steel or gut,
a job he can do with his one eye closed.

Yet his mother is so proud. He can't bear
to describe the castle—gray walls gone bare,
tapestries torn for rags by some past king;
the royal bowling alley, long since closed,
with its last seven-ten split. Trying to
learn his favorites, the blind cook tests his gut

with salty pie after pie. He is loved

by his subjects but he knows it's dog-love,
the hand licked so it will scratch. They are bears
dancing for bread because the sack of guts
is out of reach. The sack of guts, now king.

His eye whips bookies and bankers into
honesty, aligns the maps, tailors clothes.

He debunks monsters, declares cases closed,
deciphers elephants. He tries to love
the small permissions: adding an hour to
Fridays, his mom's chauffeur, appointing bears

the State Police of Twilight. They say kings

are born to rule, power grown in their guts
by childhood frictions. But in this king's gut
churns loneliness he can only disclose
to his coy and courtly dates. When the king

blinks the world goes dark. Stocks fall. So he loves
what is safe to love. Pirouetting bears,
strutting peacocks, the kangaroos bounced two
by two toward his high throne. Who is he to
demand baser thrills? But he recalls gut
strings, thrumming, almost more than he can bear—

her upright and maple body, hewn closed

except for that wide, singing mouth, a love
cradled between his feet. Among the kings

the one-eyed man goes blind. *Don't get too close,*
his gut growls. What a man hungers to love

makes him a bear. What he bears makes him king.

ECONOMY

After he has surrendered to pillows
and she, that second whiskey,
on the way to bed she traces her fingers
over a thermostat they dare not turn up.
He has stolen what they call the *green thing*—
too thick to be a blanket, too soft to be a rug—
turned away, mid-dream. Yet his legs
still reach for her legs, folding them quick
to his accumulated heat.
                    These days
only a word can earn overtime.
Economy: once a net, now a handful of holes.
Economy: what a man moves with
when, even in sleep, he is trying to save
all there is left to save.

PARABLE

Worries come to a man and a woman.
Small ones, light in the hand.

The man decides to swallow his worries,
hiding them deep within himself. The woman
throws hers as far as she can from their porch.
They touch each other, relieved.
They make coffee, and make plans for
the seaside in May.
                    All the while, the worries
of the man take his insides as their oyster,
coating themselves in juice—first gastric,
then nacreous—growing layer upon layer.
And in the fields beyond the wash-line,
the worries of the woman take root,
stretching tendrils through the rich soil.

The parable tells us *Consider the ravens,*
but the ravens caw useless from the gutters
of this house. The parable tells us
Consider the lilies, but they shiver in the side-yard,
silent.
          What the parable does not tell you

is that this woman collects porcelain cats.
Some big, some small, some gilded, some plain.
One stops doors. One cups cream and another, sugar.
This man knows they are tacky. Still, when the one
that had belonged to her great-aunt fell
and broke, he held her as she wept, held her
even after her breath had lengthened to sleep.

The parable does not care about such things.

Worry has come to the house of a man
and a woman. Their garden yields greens gone
bitter, corn cowering in its husk.
He asks himself, *What will we eat?* They sit
at the table and open the mail: a bill, a bill, a bill,
an invitation. She turns a saltshaker cat
between her palms and asks, *What will we wear?*
He rubs her wrist with his thumb.
He wonders how to offer
the string of pearls writhing in his belly.

FIDELITY (I)

She did not mean to keep the whisk
when she packed the kitchen
of the apartment they once lived in.

Night after night he'd tried to emulsify
soy sauce and peanut butter
with a fork,
before dumping the tanbrown mess on lettuce
and chicken breasts boiled to lumps,
good fat bubbling off
to pool in the hollow of the burner.

The whisk was an honest gift,
curlicued in white-ridged ribbon—
from a woman who trusted
overpriced solutions,
to a man who thought
anything could blend
if he worked his hand hard enough.

THE TRAVELER'S VADE MECUM, LINE #5450: "IN A STATE OF INTOXICATION"

The navel corresponds to the omphalos.
A corner corresponds to a perpendicular.
A spoon corresponds against its bowl—
curve to curve, an efficiency of emptying.
When the ax hits an inconvenient sapling,
the wound corresponds to the strike.
When I say I wish to correspond with you,
what I mean is I want to bite your tongue
across these many miles. I was careful.
Careful did not serve me. Can the foot
correspond with a tightrope? One always
trying to outdo the other. For a year,
a black speck has floated on my right eye.
It corresponds to nothing. It is and is.
It reminds me that what I see does not
correspond to what I touch. Not anymore.

HALLOWEEN

Somewhere in town tonight,
a woman is discovering
her inner Sexy Pirate.

This is not to be confused
with one's inner Sexy Witch,
Sexy Kitten, Sexy Librarian,
Sexy Bo Peep, Sexy Vampire,
Sexy Race Car Driver, or
inner Sexy Ophthalmologist.

She forgot to buy ribbon,
so she threads the corset's eyelets
with gym shoes laces.
She re-poofs the sleeves
of her buccaneer blouse.

Arrrr, she says to the mirror.
Argh, the mirror sighs in return.

Once a daughter asked why
anyone would wear tights like that
to net a fish.

Wouldn't your legs get cold?
Wouldn't your heels slip
on the wet deck of a ship? *Shush,*

her mother said, adjusting the wig
on her Sexy Cleopatra.

Somewhere in town tonight,
a sitter sets out the pumpkin.
A girl studies its fat head.
They punch its eyes in, so
it can see. They cut its mouth out,
so it can smile. *Now you bring it*

to life, the sitter will say.
And where its seeds had been,
the girl will place a flame.

THE TRAVELER'S VADE MECUM, LINE #2485: "I HAVE NOT DECIDED"

The all-nite diner of the dead has a $5.99 flapjack special.

Sisyphus lifts the spatula but the batter keeps dissolving.

At the counter, Ixion spins the lazy Susan's parade

of hot sauce and ketchup, eternally brined Peppadews.

They pour eight Olympic swimming pools of coffee.

They slap enough bacon to circle the earth twice.

Each time Tantalus says he's taking his break,

more customers come in. They order the bottomless cup.

He'll bring you sugar and, without asking, bring you cream.

At first the hells were assembled a sheet at a time,

each brittle as a potato chip. This was costly.

We have switched to a process that uses a unified core.

Once a howl is cured with melamine, it cannot be broken.

You're always an hour away from where you said you'd be.

THE TRAVELER'S VADE MECUM, LINE #6716: "THE STRICTEST ORDER MUST BE PRESERVED"

In the Bureau of Forms, he serves as the Office
of Bacciferous Plants. He patents The Holly. He proofs
The Asparagus. By the time a blueberry Fla-Vor-Ice
has stained any tongue teal, he has seen the application
for Platonic flavor and stamped it DENIED.

He is protective in particular of The Blackberry,
which his predecessor allowed to veer slutty and thornless:
Apache, Hull, Chester, Boysenberry, Black Satin,
the bastard children of what he has sworn to uphold.

When he goes home each night, he heats a TV dinner—
not to enjoy the mushy pork or peas or potatoes mashed,
but to remind himself that what the best and the worst
have in common is that they are immutable. Still,
he longs for the crunch of good, tensed truth. He considers
a lateral transfer to the Office of Herbaceous Perennials.
The raw artichoke unfurls its fist, motions him closer.

The Traveler's Vade Mecum, Line #4646: "Vegetation Grows Rapidly"

The frantic wasp hauls herself free from the goat fruit, swollen with her sisters. They are stapled by the handful to each tree. Their paper bags are singing. Her wings tear off at the unripe hull's door. Her ovipositor thrusts, failing, as the enzymes seduce her gravid body. Their paper bags are singing. The air ripples with sugar. Each Calimyrna fig is a bloom, housed in its own stem. Slice your teeth to the nutty roe of drupelets—a bouquet left on a graveyard stone.

Entries from *The Lover's Field Guide*

If collecting nectar from a black mangrove, observe the pencil-like tubes extending upward from the root system. These shoot poison darts.

The Atlantic deer cowrie has a fawn-brown *porcellana* and big, limpid eyes.

When handling the Southern leopard frog, it is best to whip it sidearm—maximizing speed while eliciting its balloon-like chuckle. The Eastern narrow-mouthed toad can be lobbed underhand.

Amethysts are harvested from the spines of L. M. Montgomery books. They are abundant in sections describing consumptive deaths of key characters.

If shelling for angel wings do not confuse them with the American piddock, "false angel wing"—a variety of venus clam notable for its small size, lack of radial ribs, and salty vocabulary.

❦

When the temperature rises above 2,300 degrees and 60 kilobars of pressure is applied to any common household balalaika, jade is formed.

❦

Peridot is an Atlas, hoisting entire islands upon its craggy shoulders.

❦

The teenage crane fly goes through a rebellious period during which it demands to be called by its alternate name, "Mosquito Hawk."

❦

The horseshoe crab's aliases include Saucepan, Sword-tail, and Cyclops. He resents these implications. He hails from scorpions.

Tourmaline has been recreated in laboratories using packing twine and cumin.

Weasel fur lasts longer than mink, which is why nine out of ten minks choose weasel when acquiring coats for winter.

Garnets are best smuggled tucked into the hide folds of an Indian rhinoceros.

You can tell the wentletrap is carnivorous by its purple flesh, and the welcome mat it places at the foot of its turret.

The painted turtle is an unreliable narrator.

Moonstone occurs naturally in three out of five roller-skating rinks, while the dreams of horses are often mistaken for citrine.

A giant water bug is also known as a "toe-biter"; in Florida, as an "alligator tick"; in Nevada, as the "great horned whatthefuck"; in the Marais Poitevin region, as "Claude"; and in Thailand as *Maeng Daa*, with plum sauce for dipping.

400 million years in, ammonites wonder what more they can do. Check out those whorled chambers. Do you appreciate the difficulty of radial symmetry?

Owing to flexible hip joints, a marsh wren can straddle from branch to branch, cattail to cattail. He grasps a dried-out reed in each claw and, using them as chopsticks, feeds spiders into his darling's gullet.

A man itemizes all the ways he will fail his woman. If only he'd become a paramedic. If only he baked bread. He clenches his jaw. There is topaz embedded in his back molars, but he will never find it.

THE EDITOR OF *ENCYCLOPÆDIA BRITANNICA* REGRETS EVERYTHING
Edinburgh, 1772

Add this to the list of truths they did not
need: that the white fur that grows with no eyes,
no tongue, is mere cotton. *Scythian Lamb,*
they had named it, believing the beast bent
its umbilical stem to graze the fields
before turning, bleating, to its flower
pose. All God's creatures should have a flower
pose. Did they need to know the horn was not
a horn, that no uni-horse raced their fields?
Instead we gave them a crusty, cross-eyed
seawhale who studies his own tooth, the bent
bone spiral long enough to skewer a lamb.
We made shish kebab out of magic. Lamb,
forgive us. Maidens, forgive us. Your flowered
wreaths gone to waste, beloved truths bending
to guillotine fact: What was, is now not.
They call it *Enlightenment* but my eyes
see only shadows creeping down the fields,
the mothers calling tots in from the fields,
mothers now knowing all that hunts their lambs—
how many teeth, legs, claws. How many eyes.
Each *genus* and *specie* of deadly flower
grown wild in Scotland. And no, we did not

mean for our little book to take this bent—
any more than lightning means to take bent
toward the farmhouse it sets aflame, the fields
whipping orange into the night. We're not
prophets or shepherds, not looking for lambs.
We're scientists. We thought truth was a flower
waiting to be plucked by our hands and eyes.
A body dissected is, to our eyes,
the body collected. We tore roots, bent
stems, pressed petals in pages, called them *flowers*.
Measured topographies and called them *fields*.
Cut throat, shoulder, hock, and called it a *lamb*.
What I'd give, to see what lenses cannot
see. I'd trade in my eyes to run these fields
and bend my neck, as meekly as a lamb,
to flowers tied by a sweet woman's knot.

One-Tenth of the Body

The ship's steward didn't know
what he had photographed.

They looked at that smear
along the berg's base, red paint
from the *Titanic*'s hull—

and called it
>   *the wound,*

as if the North Atlantic's ice
had gashed its side in sympathy.

But they had seen only
one-tenth of the frozen body.

What they thought a shroud
no more than
>   a kerchief,

the red silk any disaster
tucks in its pocket
before stepping out to dance.

If a Metro car comes behind another
and mounts it,

that first squeal sounds
almost like
                    joy.

On the Red Line train, a man
watches the floor peel away
beneath his feet.

He knows what happens
when you set tinned fish free.

THE TRAVELER'S VADE MECUM, LINE #7405: "THE OFFER WILL NOT BE REPEATED"

Two men walk on a path.
One has a blade in his pocket.
We do not know if the edge
is grimed with paint, or butter,
or is clean as a newborn tongue.
One has an apple in his pocket.
Put a horse at the end of the path
and he is kind to animals. Leave
the horse out, and he is hungry.
They can stop and sit together,
knife licking away the skin
in perfect, blush-red strips.
One will look over his shoulder.
One will fail an appointment
he promised to keep. But they
can have this meal, if they
choose. Then keep walking.

THE TRAVELER'S VADE MECUM, LINE #614: "DO NOT EXPOSE YOURSELF TO THE AIR"

To live is to take without permission.
If you could see oaks
in their entirety, you would be offended
by their many-fingered grab of dirt and sky.

In the kitchen of the gods our mother makes
neat sandwiches, trimming cosmic crust,
layering mayo with a knife.
She's humming a tune. Her back is turned.
Every breath is a child's hand
rummaging through the bag of grapes.

Our lifespan yields to Hayflick's limit:
fifty times, plus or minus a few,
that a cell can divide before dying.
Within us, one jail becomes two jails.
Within us, two jails becomes four.

THE TRAVELER'S VADE MECUM, LINE #4088: "IN THE LATEST FASHION"

Before the woman crosses the street with her ferret, she tucks it high under her arm like an unruly baguette. We will never know if it is a hob or a jill, a sprite or a gib, or whether it opens its tiny mouth to the rain that will come on in another moment, rain we will ignore while it fills our wineglasses, rain that putters among the last of the lentils. She carries nothing else—no handbag, no umbrella. His little thief face looks up with something like loyalty. Perhaps that is what desire looks like, when you allow someone to pin the canister of your rib cage against her own. At home, my suitcase is open on a bed that is not your bed. The ferret noses at her sweater, clucking. You say my name but I would rather be her, this woman who has found her interrobang and refuses to set it down.

THE TRAVELER'S VADE MECUM,
LINE #2239: "COTTON IS RISING"

If hunting a lion, the weight of one's gaze will scare it off.
So one must always close his eyes before hunting a lion.

If he is to perform an inverse operation on the universe,
the hunter must be sure to step inside the cage beforehand.

The sky can have its Orion.
On this night, he hovers with a girl in a field of astral spunk.

Because he wants to be touched, he does not touch her.
Because she wants to be caught, she will run.

THE TRAVELER'S VADE MECUM, LINE #2437: "YOUR DAUGHTER HAS NOT LEFT"

Don't bother checking the tower.
Don't split the belly of the wolf.
She chews twigs, not grass;
rind, not berry.
She does not go underground.
She goes 45 mph.
Animalia:
Chordata:
Mammalia:
Lagomorpha:
Leporidae:
Lepus. Jill
to your Jack,
Jack to your Jack:
her realm one of precision.
Beyond a pair, in droves.
Alone? Driven.
Zoologists call hers
the *kinetic skull*—
shifting so even
her bones absorb the jump.
Mad as March.
Sadder than. Name
what you aim to warm with touch.

VALENTINE FOR THE GRAVE DIGGER

Tell her it's not the oldest job, but close.
Fossor, from Latin's *fodere,* the dark
art of structured loss. Or as she thinks, *Holes.*
Don't rhapsodize the sod's sigh, the liftoff,
the two-step of digging and herding dirt.
Ask her if she's heard of the monster truck;
when in doubt, chicks dig a sweet monster truck.
If it's not what first comes to mind, it's close.
Next she might ask what you find in the dirt:
Tabasco, dimes, a six-pack of Beck's Dark,
hand-drawn Ouija boards. Teenagers run off,
leaving their joints. One mourner left a whole
golf bag with clubs, as if the nineteenth hole
was heaven. You keep it all in your truck.
Don't try to impress her by listing off
other diggers—Richie Hebner, who closed
batting .301 and, diamond gone dark,
returned to summer in his father's dirt;
or Abraham Lincoln, down in the dirt
of Little Pigeon Cemetery, holes
being the sexton's duty. In the dark
flatbed comforts of a good man's pickup,
Lincoln won't get you laid. Not even close.

Mention Joe Strummer, singing on and off
for the Vultures while earning his rent off
of corpses. Maybe she'll go for that. Dirt
is a great excuse for taking off clothes.
You know fifteen ways to talk about holes.
Builds bulk, loading and unloading a truck.
Builds instinct, working blinded by the dark.
Tonight's pretty woman waits in the dark
with glittered skin. Pretend it's her night off.
Pretend that she likes you. Not that you'd truck
in gossip but, face it, you get the dirt
on us all in the end. She's a black hole.
She's all yours if you keep your wallet close.
Or? Run to me, your Alice of dark dirt,
offering my hand toward the Rabbit Hole.
I'm just a truck crash away. You're so close.

American Caution

Twenty years in and we keep slowing
for the Blind Child at Play
who now—a Blind Wife, a Blind Mother—
makes spaghetti on the other side of town.
Still, we heed. We fasten. We brake.
Though the barn has slumped to ash,
a promise of cows roam the mountain fog.
Flick your brights. A gang of elk
will cross the road, any minute now.
Wait for it.
                    Consider, when
they offer to name a day in a man's honor,
the ten thousand days to follow.
These will be, by definition, not his days.
If you purchase a Celestial Registration Kit
your sweetheart's star will outlive her
in that distant galaxy, flexing light in hope
of a constellation's embrace.
We record with echo chambers—
the oil-can delay, the Pythian Temple,
the microphone in the toilet—
because, without the familiar distortions,
no one believes the sound they hear.

To a fairground goldfish, the good toss
doesn't feel like victory.
He sees only an apocalypse,
the flagrant moon hurtling down for a kiss.

GRIEF PUPPET

In the nearby plaza, musicians would often gather.
The eternal flame was fueled by propane tank.
An old man sold chive dumplings from a rolling cart,
while another grilled skewers of paprika beef.
Male turtledoves would puff their breasts, *woo*-ing,
and for a few coins, we each bought an hour with
the grief puppet. It had two eyes, enough teeth,
a black tangle of something like hair or fur,
a flexible spine that ran the length of your arm.
Flick your wrist, and at the end of long rods
it raised its hands as if conducting the weather.
Tilt the other wrist, and it nodded. No effort
was ever lost on its waiting face. It never
needed a nap or was too hungry to think straight.
You could have your conversation over and over,
past dusk when old men doused their charcoal,
into rising day when they warmed their skillets.
The puppet only asked what we could answer.
Some towns had their wall, others their well;
we never gave the stupid thing a name, nor
asked the name of the woman who took our coins.
But later, we could all remember that dank felt,
and how the last of grief's flock lifted from our chests.

THE TRAVELER'S VADE MECUM, LINE #1181: "THE CALAMITY IS NOT SERIOUS"

He catches the rain in his cooking pot.
There's nothing to put in his cooking pot.
He places a stone in his cooking pot.
He dances by the fire as the water boils.

"Stone soup, stone soup," he sings.
"Lend a little garnish," he tells our village,

"soon you'll each have a bowl."
In go the carrot-tops, the rosemary,
in goes the hambone with larded lips.
The children gather. The strays mewl.

Sometimes it has to be button soup.
Sometimes ax soup, sometimes nail.

In France he is a soldier, in Portugal
he is a monk stirring *sopa de pedra*.
Wherever he goes he is The Clever Man:
Folktale 1548 in the Aarne-Thompson index.

Not to be confused with his brothers
Eulenspiegel (1635), Master Thief (1525),

or 1574, The Flattering Foreman.
He'll never have a turn as The Stupid Man,
The Man Looking for a Wife,
or The Man Who Kills (Injures) Ogre.

His is not the Cat as Helper (545B).
His will never be The Lucky Accident.

He wakes each day with an empty pot
and the spoon his grandmother gave him.
"Stone soup, stone soup," he sings.
The heel on his left boot loosens, so

he dances harder. Our village is his pantry.
His is the recipe that needs no knife.

THE TRAVELER'S VADE MECUM, LINE #8289: "MILLS HAVE STOPPED FOR WANT OF WATER"

I followed the others, taking a week's wage to raise
Potemkin's town. Up go three steeples, up go garlands.
No bread, yet a man bellows smoke from the bakery.
No children, yet a thatch on the schoolhouse roof.
Under the skin of each haystack seethes a pile of
broken wagon beds, spent axles. Night's garlic fires
make the last thin horse stamp nervously in his stall.
We have named the horse Grigory. We watch his
terrific eyes swivel. They see everything except
what lies immediately ahead and behind them,
which means that in the beat before a horse jumps,
the obstacle drops away. If Grigory dies,
we are to still lean his body against the fence.
I will write you, but I will not write these things.
There is no trusted address for reply.
No smiling here, only the grin of bared teeth
facing the river where our Empress will soon pass by.

The Traveler's Vade Mecum, Line #4234: "Flour Is Firm"

Baking two parts flour to one part water
could stop a bullet. So good soldiers
carried their hardtack over their hearts.
Break it down with a rifle butt, flood it,
fry it in pig fat to make hellfire stew.
Gnaw it raw and praise the juice.

Does wheat prepare for this as it grows,
seeking the light in a half-thawed field?
Do stalks know their strength is merely
in their number? What is ground down
we name *flour* in promise that it will be
made useful. Otherwise, it's just dust.

Sheet iron crackers.
Teeth-dullers.
Would you call it starving, if a man dies
with hardtack still tucked in his vest?
Can you call it food, if the bullet comes only
at the moment he gives in and swallows?

The Psychology Lesson

Trace the path through Phineas Gage's skull
where a three-foot, seven-inch tamping rod shot
under the cheek, behind the left eye, and out,
taking his frontal lobe with it. Yet he lived.

Life is stubborn. Shatter a mind and the fragments
rename themselves Vicky or Peggy Ann, find
a doll to clutch.
                        The narcoleptic dachshund
tries to waddle the long hall to his food bowl.
Though his body is beached by waves of sleep,
he wakes hopeful every time, famished.

Meet the hypothalamus: *hungry, horny, happy.*
What drives us is the constellation of nuclei.
What drives us is the size of an almond.

The psych teacher herds us into the boys' bathroom,
where each student is told to grab a urinal handle.
Pull, she commands. Water rushes rushes
rushesrushesrushesrushes   roars
—splash guards crest—
                        everyone, it's beautiful—

but before the toilets are ready she commands
Pull again.   No draw.   We yank and yank,
helpless, as she explains the refractory period

of orgasm. We're good students. We ace the test.
It'll be years before we lay a hand to someone's skin
without feeling cold, sticky steel; years to learn
that pleasure is a reflex neither pathetic nor finite.

There were reports the rod whistled as it flew.
A scientist modeled the trajectory, and swore
Phineas's mouth had been open, that the open mouth
had saved him. He met the first doctor, and said,
Here's business enough for you. Phrenologists would say
his organ of veneration had been destroyed—
that his brain had no loyalty or adoration left.
But we have seen the photographs:
his neatly slicked hair and his buttoned vest.
For the rest of his life, Phineas carried that iron.

UKULELE

The vessel is simple, a rowboat among yachts.

No one hides a Tommy gun in its case.

No bluesman runs over his uke in a whiskey rage.

The last of the Hawai'ian queens translated the name

gift that came here, while Portuguese historians translate

jumping flea, the way a player's fingers pick and fly.

If you have a cigar box, it'll do. If you have fishing line,

it'll sing. If there is to be one instrument of love—

not love vanished or imagined, but love—it's this one.

Fit a melody in the crook of your arm, and strum.

Let Me Count the Waves

We must not look for poetry in poems.
—Donald Revell

You must not skirt the issue wearing skirts.
You must not duck the bullet using ducks.
You must not face the music with your face.
Headbutting, don't use your head. Or your butt.
You must not use a house to build a home,
and never look for poetry in poems.

In fact, inject giraffes into your poems.
Let loose the circus monkeys in their skirts.
Explain the nest of wood is not a home
at all, but a blind for shooting wild ducks.
Grab the shotgun by its metrical butt;
aim at your Muse's quacking, Pringled face.

It's good we're talking like this, face to face.
There should be more headbutting over poems.
Citing an '80s brand has its cost but
honors the teenage me, always in skirts,
showing my sister how to Be the Duck
with a potato-chip beak. Take me home,

Mr. Revell. Or make yourself at home
in my postbellum, Reconstruction face—

Instantaneous Letter Writer

After the others go to bed, my lamp
the only light for six miles,
they return:
                    a crowd of moths
who wreathe my window's panes
before making their way in,
batting their songs along the ceiling
and eventually on my book, my cup,
my arm. I could shove each husk
on a hook, cast him out—
a final descent
worthy of a Mardi Gras prince.
Or press them to the resin of my veins
so when they split the tree of my body
they'd be chiseled free;
reborn, framed in sterling.
                              Instead
each keeps buzzing in his crumpled tissue,
Plácido Domingo
in the amphitheater of my wastebasket.
To weaken one's grip as you crush a thing
is not the same as mercy.

my gray eyes, my rebel ears, all my ducks
in the row of a defeated mouth. Poems
were once civil. But war has torn my skirts
off at the first ruffle, baring my butt

or as termed in verse, my luminous butt.
Whitman once made a hospital his home.
Emily built a prison of her skirts.
Tigers roamed the sad veldt of Stevens's face.
That was the old landscape. All the new poems
map the two dimensions of cartoon ducks.

We're young and green. We're braces of mallards,
not barrels of fish. Shoot if you must but
Donald, we're with you. Trying to save poems,
we settle and frame their ramshackle homes.
What is form? Building art from artifice,
trading pelts for a more durable skirt.

Even urban ducklings deserve a home.
Make way. In the modern: *Make way, Buttface.*
A poem's coming through, lifting her skirt.

THE TRAVELER'S VADE MECUM, LINE #6833: "THE PEOPLE BEGIN TO UNDERSTAND"

The line joining two points on a curve defines a chord.

Curves may be concave or convex, a gathering or dispersion.

You don't know until you know which side you stand on.

Once, a man paid to put the two of us in a hot air balloon.

We didn't know the words to the song, but we were trying

to hum the chords anyway. We lifted above the earth.

Fields and farms raced below us. I wish he'd paid extra.

For extra, they drop the earth away as you stay where you are.

THE TRAVELER'S VADE MECUM, LINE #346: "THE BANKS HAVE BEGUN TO CONTRACT"

One bridge, a hare's leap over the Monongahela—
One, a hawk's low swoop along the Allegheny—
One a Hot Metal truss, one a strung bow,

three Sisters suspended and a terminus at Liberty—
If you count the bridges of this city, you lose count.
This is not what we'd planned. A city should grow

like a muscle. We'll flex until the small fibers rip,
bathe in the amino acid's flood. Only a child
tries to staple a tear in the lifting shoulder of God.

THE SWORD SWALLOWER'S VALENTINE

You had me at that martini. I saw
you thread the olive's red pimento throat
with your plastic swizzle stick, a deft act
at once delicate and greedy. A man
who is paid to taste the blade knows his match.
The pleasure. The brine. *I wish we had time,*
I said—you stopped me—*There's always time.*
That's when they called me to the stage. I saw
your mouth's angle change as you made a match
of my name and *Noted Gullet! Steel Throat!*
Ramo Swami, the Sword-Swallowing Man.
I want to assure you it's just an act,
but since age seven it's the only act
I know. My mother recalls that first time
she caught my butter-knife trick: a real man
might not cry, but the real boy wept. She saw
my resolve to build a tunnel from throat
to feet. *A dark that deep could go unmatched,*
she warned. Your smile is the strike of a match,
the hope of an inner spelunking act.
Facing the crowd, the sight of your pale throat
tightens mine at the worst possible time—
that fickle tic of desire. *Yeah, I saw*

his last show, you'll say. *Lost focus, poor man.*
Funny how women make and break their men,
how martinis both break and make a match.
The best magician will hang up his saw,
release his doves, if the right woman acts
to un-straitjacket his body in time.
If lips meet, the hint of gin in your throat
will mingle with camellia in my throat,
same oil used by any samurai man.
I trained against touch once upon a time,
not knowing a rigid pharynx would match
a rigid heart. I'm ready to react,
to bleed. As any alchemist can see,
to fill a throat with raw steel is no match
for love. Don't clap for these inhuman acts.
Cut me in two. Time, time: the oldest saw.

THE CIRCUS

Henri de Toulouse-Lautrec

❧

In the halls of Pigalle, juxtaposition is not intimacy.
Moulin Rouge Moulin Rouge Moulin
Red—Louise the Glutton spread high in her kick,

boneless Valentin a gray foreground shimmy.
The hedge of suitors stomp their feet, whistling,
as Henri leans into another absinthe.

Later he'll plot the scene in fatty crayon
before washing the limestone with gum arabic.
In lithography, beauty is born when attraction

and repulsion work together. He wearies the rut
to accept ink. He applies even, unyielding pressure,
until the poultice of paper cannot help

but stanch the wound. Black; yellow; blue.
He must match registers or one color outgrows
the other, the story blurring. His right thigh

fractured at thirteen. The left, at fourteen.
When cousin seduces cousin, the gods give them
a satyr son—full torso and a boy's faltering legs,

a goat's humor and a kid's sex. He knifes
the brush's edge for a silver spatter. He celebrates
lips painted in carmine, the perfect stink of an armpit.

In the halls of Pigalle he watches Jane hoist her knee
to the ceiling joists, her black glove a hummingbird
darting into her skirt's bloom, and the bassist

chokes higher on the neck of his instrument.
For the camera, Henri wears Jane's boa, her ostrich hat.
He will pose as Pierrot, as a gossamered choir boy,

as Muslim cleric, as Japanese princess with doll.
Why not? His gift: able to see every nature
beneath decoration. His curse: unable to change it.

At the Cirque Fernando the ringmaster offers
his whip to the bareback rider, her dappled horse
galloping toward a squat clown with a paper circle.

The red of their lips kiss across the air. This
is the first painting of his they hung at the Rouge.
A canvas three times its height waited at the studio,

a promise he could not keep. His days ran dusk to dawn,
poster to poster to poster, and now he draws his pistol
to shoot spiders. Sores spread, gut corroded.

His mother herds him like an animal to the asylum
of Neuilly-sur-Seine. He bucks and brays at the cage
before realizing, like any animal, the hoop he must jump.

Chalk; charcoal; crayon. He circumscribes each page in
empty stands. Here there is no cheering bourgeoisie
guillotined by the paper's edge. He admits no audience

to see the Jacob's Ladder of the equestrienne's spine
or the tamer, prostrate below a rearing stallion
whose ears lay back, his nostrils flared.

The performers eye each other. They flex and sweat.
He plays the sinews of muscle like a harp,
plucks harmony in palette: it is the same blue

clothing the clown as the ribbon on the dog's head,
same blue hide of the elephant who raises a tired leg
as he balances on pedestal and smokes a cigar.

For Arsène Alexandre—A souvenir of my captivity—
Thirty-nine times Henri returns to Montmartre's rings.
Doctors gather, marveling at such perfect recollection.

Sanity is judged not by your story, but the telling of it.
He dreams of the embrace of carborundum grit
that cleans the limestone, that lets us begin again.

THE TRAVELER'S VADE MECUM, LINE #6459: "THE COUNTRY IS QUITE MOUNTAINOUS"

The goats of Kaua'i care little for our taxonomies.
No one has told them they are not mountain goats.
No one has shown them the logs of Captain Cook,
who seeded their ancestors with a casual hand;
no one has spoken of how the villagers stabbed him,
face down in the surf, before baking his skeleton
free of flesh. The goats gambol and bray on the cliffs.
They do not stop at dirt. They chew to the root.
We watch them from our little ship, floating in
a bigger blue thing they have no name for, under
the pull of our hot daily something. But these goats,
they orbit nothing. They move no way but forward.

THE TRAVELER'S VADE MECUM,
LINE #2484: "I HAVE DECIDED"

In Ashley's *Book of Knots*, he called it the Oysterman's Stopper.
You form an overhand noose, thread the working end and
tighten. No matter how you pull, the trefoil will turn away. But
the trawler-men Ashley credited—should we have clambered
their decks—would have shown us only an everyday figure-
eight knot, swollen with salt of a thousand waves. Ruin is always
a form of invention. When the shark's corpse washes ashore and
people see the scapulocoracoids, horns once hidden under fins,
they murmur *Dragon*. The knot you tied did not fail. It was
designed to follow us, shapely, down this length of rope.

INVENTORY

We gaze into your eyes, eyes, eyes, eyes.
We forget the display is blind.

Your fanned tail really a cupped palm,
gathering each hen's quiver to your ear,

your feathers the greenblue glamours
of reflective absence. No one

ever praises the ass of the peacock,
grin of quills that does the heavy lifting,

or how you eat anything from ants
to Styrofoam, from cheese to chicken.

Road roamer, flower devourer:
the one who'll pick a fight with a goat.

Preen all you want. What I praise of you
will be the bare undercarriage,

the calamus. I am done with beauty.
Only a blinking eye can measure the light.

THE TRAVELER'S VADE MECUM, LINE #8206 "WHAT IS THE WHOLESALE PRICE OF THE TRAVELER'S VADE MECUM?"

I intend to converse with many. None in the same room.
I have a daughter to search for, an acre of farmland to sell.
I must confirm that flour is falling and copper is rising;
I must offer my compliments to the ladies.
I will be refusing all medical advice, except for that
of gentlemen known for punctuality. Where can I find you
in this city? This parish? In this Gypsy market with dirt floors?

If some think me babbling, imagine how a game of chess
appears to one who has only ever known a checkerboard.

I own one suit for going south and another for going under.
I traveled before I was born, and will travel after I die.
They will come together, each clutching their copies,
and raid my library. Beside *Your love is reciprocated*,
they will find four tickmarks. Beside *I am fond of loneliness*,
they will find fifteen. A wrought-iron gate makes beautiful
not its bars, but the spaces between its bars. Without structure

there can be no mystery. Dear sirs, thank you for this service.
You have shaken down the Garden of Eden for its seeds.